Printed in the United States of America

First Printing: November 2015

HUNTER HERITAGE PUBLISHING

ISBN-13: 978-0692561454

ISBN-10: 0692561455

Cover Design By: Andrea M.V. Hunter – Diop

Editing By: Andrea M.V. Hunter – Diop

Immigration Dating and Marriage:

~ Love, Leverage, Loss ~

An Informative Guide on Immigration Exploitation, Scams Involving Dating, Love and Marriage in America

Andrea M.V. Hunter – Diop

This book is dedicated with love and affection to: My sons, George Michael and Lamine (R.I.P) And to my parents, Linda Marie and Ronald F. Hunter, Sr. whom loved, nurtured, guided and tried to protect me from the ills of the world.

~~~~~~

Also in dedication are those that I have dated, loved and married whom served as the inspiration for this book and a call to action to help protect others from Immigration Exploitation and Scams Involving Dating, Love and Marriage.

A Word from Andrea M.V. Hunter - Diop

They say lightening doesn't strike twice. Well I can tell you different. Before the age of 40 years old, I had been legally married twice, divorced once and am currently estranged. Both of my husbands were illegal immigrants when I met them, unbeknownst to me at the time. I sponsored both for green card visa's resulting in their citizenship, as United States citizens by naturalization.

While I love and loved both my husbands - I loved them differently. But the hurt I experienced was the same. The experiences of both marriages have served as a catalyst for this cathartic written work, be it small as it may. It is my hope that my book will shine light on the often silent, systemic problem of Immigration marriage fraud - that is often overlooked and over shadowed by Immigration reform pertaining to other areas of interest and terrorism.

The content herein is not a smear campaign against immigrants drawn from conjecture or a libelous account of my marriages to slander my husbands. Nor is my writing from the perspective of a detracted xenophobe.

This book of the self –help genre, is drawn from my experiences and the experiences of others that have been exploited through relationship and marriage fraud. It is my aim to take a swipe at immigration exploitation and marriage fraud through recognition of the motives, the agenda and behavioral cues exhibited by some immigrants for their personal profit in obtaining a green card visa and citizenship.

Often I replayed interactions with my husbands "things said and done" in my mind, over and over – wondering what did I miss. How did

I end up here, not once but twice??!! It was through this process of analyzation that I was able to recognize the symptomatic behavioral cues and identify the **4 C's - choice**, **chance**, **change** and **control which will be explained throughout the chapters**.

This book is also a call to action, to help protect others from Immigration Exploitation and Scams Involving Dating, Love and Marriage by being able to identify and anticipate specific behavioral cues.

In the event, that you – like me, learned too little too late that you were defrauded into marriage for personal profit and gain by Immigration Fraud you too can benefit from this read.

You can learn how to be an advocate for yourself, heal the hurt and move past the pain. Go from being a victim to a victor and become better not bitter.

CONTENTS

ONE - IMMIGRANT ITELLIGENCE

You may find you're looking for someone to love and someone to **_love_** you – as love is not ubiquitous. Some immigrants will use this very basic human need of love as **_leverage_** to exploit you for a Immigration Green Card Visa and/or Citizenship sponsorship and once their Immigration need, want is met you most likely will be disposed of which will put you in a position of **_loss_** of what you thought the dynamic of your relationship was, what the true dynamic and basis of your relationship is or was.

This book will serve as a guide for both men and women to discern and gauge behavioral cues, the deleterious deeds of an "in need immigrant" that you plan on being involved with or are romantically involved with.

Often many forms of deceptive behaviors; relationship and marriage scams and behavioral cues will vary based on the country of origin and will often be influenced by cultural, religious and individual factors.

In any regard, this book will serve to make you privy to their motives, agenda, methodical thinking and the behavioral cues so you can exercise informed decision making while navigating through courting, dating and marriage with a "in need immigrant".

I use the term "in need immigrant" because not all immigrants are illegal or motive driven, however as with anyone or anything there are particular parasitic sectors of bad.

This guide speaks to that particular population of immigrants that are in need of an immigration status change and are willing to use, hurt and defraud people genuinely looking for love – that is to be loved and give love into relationships, marriages for the sole purpose of obtaining a visa and/or citizenship, thus raising their own personal profile.

For many immigrants the fantasy with America is conceptualized and begins before ever arriving abroad. The cultural melting pot that is America and the cornucopia of opportunities: education, health care, housing, employment, business opportunities and the religious freedom(s) is the lure for many Immigrants. And why many immigrants have the ideology that America is the land of opportunity.

The fantasy of America and the opportunities afforded in the U.S is often embedded in movies, music, fashion, food and by family, friends already living in America.

This rational isn't far off; as the opportunities here in the United States aren't always accessible or attainable in their country of origin. Many immigrants are impecunious in their homeland - hence, the mass migration of immigrants into America.

The motives for some immigrants to enter the U.S are: financial freedom and opportunity, work, religious freedom, political freedom, freedom from Countries of Civil unrest or reunification with family, friends inclusive of lost loves which all contribute to having a better life abroad in the U.S.

Polygamy is practiced in some immigrant communities – as a matter of culture and religion. This is particularly true in the Islamic religion of faith. For some countries of origin of immigrants; it is commonality for a man to have more than one woman that he takes as his concubine or wife - sometimes having up to 4 women that he takes as his wives though these unions are often only acknowledged in cultural, religious observances and are not legally recognized. Polyandry, in which a woman has multiple husbands, is rare.

It is important that you are aware of the specific country of origin and the cultural, religious influences of their people, as you date.

The motives, motivation for some immigrants is so great that some immigrants will migrate illegally when opportunity for legal entry is not a viable explorable option. Many immigrants enter the U.S *legally* through <u>temporary</u> visa programs, such as: work study programs, employer sponsorship or with a visiting visa. Some modes of *temporary* visa issuances for immigrants looking to enter the U.S legally are: Summer Camp Employment and student visa's (inclusive of schools that only teach students the English language and reading, writing skills). I had the experience of finding out late into one of my relationships, that one of my then boyfriends (later on, husband) had entered the U.S legally on two separate occasions using the fore-mentioned visa filings.

And some immigrants choose to enter the country *illegally*. For either the legal or illegal immigrant, often the next phase of their methodical thinking is "**How do I stay in the U.S permanently**" when renewal of their visa or all other avenues of opportunity, visas are exhausted.

That's where you come into position - <u>the position you play, **victim** or **victor** is on you and the immigrant intelligence you cultivate when it comes to dating, romance, love and marriage with an immigrant.</u>

More often than not; immigrants will often be privy to immigration and migration programs, including temporary and permanent visa programs, immigration and migration statutes and laws. ***They use this knowledge with tactical precision to know, exercise their rights and exploit yours.***

The lengths some immigrants will go to stay in the U.S are immeasurable and unfathomable. I've heard stories of female immigrants claiming that they would be victims of clitoral mutilation as a way of defrauding the U.S government body of Immigration into asylum status – when clitoral mutilation isn't performed in their country. I've heard stories of false claims of refugee status by immigrants to obtain asylum. I've heard of both male and female immigrants altering the visa photos of deceased relatives. I've heard stories of immigrants working under the identity of a friend or family member who has papers (a green card visa) legally. I've heard stories of false allegations of religious persecution by immigrants to obtain a visa. And the stories could go on and on.

As the stories of Immigration fraud escalate, so does the desperation of the immigrant to commit a nefarious caper inclusive of: marriage fraud to stay in the U.S by any means necessary.

For the fore-mentioned reasons; you must stay vigilant in protecting your heart and your sponsoring status of a green card visa and/or citizenship until you are sure you involved with the right person and for the right reasons with the exclusion of Immigration exploitation via dating, love and marriage. This means not being afraid to listen to your inner voice when something seems amiss and aberrant with your special someone.

You must be able to challenge your special someone with acerbic appropriate questioning when needed. But most importantly, loving yourself and respecting yourself enough not to let your insecurities, vulnerabilities void you of your worth so that you are not put into a precarious position of compromise.

Often immigrants are adroit in knowing the who's, what's and the how's – when it comes to looking for an ideal candidate to date and hopefully marry for exploitation when it comes to green card and citizenship sponsorship. These people are very cunning and assimilate well in most settings.

When an employer is looking to hire a specific for a position to facilitate growth, productivity and to meet the needs of the employer - there is a screening process for the ideal *candidate*. The same is true when an immigrant is looking to scam a person into a parasitic relationship for profit and exploitation. And this process also begins by selecting the ideal candidate.

Personal preferences of physical attributes, educational level, economic status, religious affiliation, family structure and even the race of an ideal candidate for immigration relationship and marriage fraud are often over looked. What is of heightened importance is finding someone who is ideally gregarious and not aloof, thus getting someone to *yes* to their advances, when others have said *no* and cultivating the acquaintance into something *seemingly* **of substance**.

Immigration exploitation through romantic relationships and marriage isn't biased based upon age, as long as you are of "legal age" to marry within your state without parental consent (the legal age requirement without parental consent will vary by state, but the general consensus of legal age to marry without parental consent is 18 years old). My first marriage was at the tender age of 18 years old to a man over 10 years my senior. Immigration exploitation also isn't gender biased – as, men are victimized by these scams just as women are and the rates aren't disproportional.

Reading this might hurt but - the ideal immigration fraud candidate is often beleaguered in a plethora of <u>perceived</u> *or* <u>real</u> – flaws and challenges, that might be inclusive of: being older, corpulent, unattractive, socially inept, introverted and/or a single parent. I've heard stories of disabled persons with health problems - physical and/or mental health issues being preyed upon, used as pawns in obtaining a green card visa and/or citizenship. Often, the fore-mentioned types of people have self - esteem, insecurity issues and are sometimes isolated. And in some cases, once a relationship has been established an "in need immigrant" will isolate you from family and friends as a form of ***control***.

It is important to note that affluent, social people aren't exempt from immigration exploitation and can also be victims of relationship immigration fraud as well. Additionally; such affluent, social, connected people of means would be an ideal candidate over the fore-mentioned types described above – especially if you own a business that can sponsor them through employer sponsorship and/or pay the exorbitant immigration filing fees.

Finding vulnerability in a candidate no matter their physical appearance, education level, financial status or social standing is important and key in adaption, assimilation of the immigrant being able to exploit you and emotions by being seemingly what you want or need in a relationship.

Once the makings of a mark (a candidate) have been made with insecurities and vulnerable characteristics exposed often; the formulating of a plan of exploitation and execution of the plan is put in place. Next the immigrant must ponder where to meet such a person. The allowable time and desperation of the immigrant is often the determiner of the pace of relationship – rarely does the relationship go at an andante pace. The selection of a candidate and viable venues to meet such a candidate are anything but arbitrary.

Much thought is put into the process - everything assiduous, methodical and calculating. Often these plans are put in place prior to arrival in the United States or soon after arrival. Family, friends of the immigrant often act as a supporting cast and interject their advisement as to how have the plan go off without a hitch once a viable candidate has been identified and a venue of meeting has been set. Often the immigrant may have a relative or friend or friend of a friend who has profited from marriage fraud in obtaining their green card and/or citizenship. Sometimes the relative or friend or friend of a friend will offer information. This information will entail how to proceed in a romantic relationship or the immigration visa sponsorship filing process and interview process by Immigration officials.

Sometimes immigrants will go as far as conducting research, reading literature as how to exhibit ardor, fervent feelings that gnaws at the emotions and attrition of the prospective candidate till they willingly capitulate. Once the inhibitions are gone, the challenge is gone and the duplicity begins. The unassuming candidate now becomes baited prey for exploitation.

Now that the components of motives, motivation, candidates for exploitation have been explained it is time to delve – into where to meet such a person, I mean mark (candidate).

TWO - PEOPLE, PLACES OF OPPORTUNITY

As discussed in the previous chapter, a specific person of interest is needed as a candidate for immigration relationship and marriage exploitation. Now that we know the types of people that are sought after, we can now explore places of opportunity that can lead to such an encounter.

Meeting people and places of opportunity is a _matter of the 4 C's_: **choice**, **chance**, **change** and **control**. The **choice** candidate leads to a seemingly **chance** meeting can ultimately **change** your life for better or worse, and take away your **control** to react appropriately. To reiterate, becoming a **_victim_** or **_victor_** is a matter of choice when controlling your emotions, the pace of the relationship and discretion in discerning who you meet and their motives, if any - when meeting.

America being built upon the backs of immigrant labor through migration, through blood, sweat and tears is still a cultural melting pot. Throughout any town, any city, any state in the U.S.A – you can and will encounter an immigrant, a _legal_ or _illegal_ immigrant but never less an immigrant. The car service industry (taxi's,cabs), restaurants, independent stores (I.E: 99 cent stores, beauty supplies, deli's/bodega's etc.), construction and domestic industries (baby sitters,house cleaners) have high influx rates of immigrant labor, be it legal or illegal. As with any daily activity, patronizing the fore-mentioned industries and establishments puts you at an increased rate to encounter a legal or illegal immigrant.

You'd be surprised how many illegal immigrants would risk losing their job for the benefit of meeting an unassuming American that they could potentially defraud into marriage and become sponsored by. The depths of desperation of the "in need immigrant" know no bounds.

For some people born and raised in America or reared in a large city such as New York, Los Angeles or Chicago – may have a false sense of security that because of the fore-mentioned, they are impregnable to immigration exploitation through dating and marriage. But as, previously discussed immigration exploitation and marriage fraud, know no bounds of bias.

Often unassuming in appearance (example: glasses - you know the nerdy type) and in some cases, unattractive - the "in need immigrant" will seek out people and places of opportunity to find a candidate to exploit.

Mundane outings on public transportation, such as the bus and/or subway also offer a place of prey when meeting a prospective candidate. Masses of people itinerant in confined spaces coming and going or awaiting the next mode of transportation – often, offer an ideal setting to be approached with unsolicited conversation. Some "in need immigrants" will also go to the gym to meet a mark (a candidate), particularly a corpulent one. Coffee shops, cafés and the library are often reserved for the intellectual "in need immigrant" but to be candid – all immigrants have some form of intellectual intelligence when exploiting the vulnerabilities of others for personal profit and gain, so you must be diligent to counter their actions.

As the song goes by Whodini, "Freaks Come Out At Night" - bars, night clubs and lounges offer a venue for your vulnerability to be exploited. The religious leaders such as: Imam's, Rabbi's, Deacon's, Priest's and Pastors etcetera of the "in need immigrant" would find it incredulous that they would frequent, patronize such a seedy establishments to a seek partner where alcohol flows free and the people are often loud, loose. While it may seem paradoxical and be hard for religious leaders to fathom the reasons to patronize such establishments that deviate from religious teachings - for the self-serving "in need immigrant" the reasons are quite clear. As, I met my second husband, a native West African and presumable devout Muslim at an American night club that serves alcohol.

The ambiance of dark lights and alcohol offer an ease of inhibitions, as personal preferences of physical attributes are put on pause. While this environment offers an inviting environment for meeting a candidate and in some cases, a desperado – it doesn't offer a quiet, intimate place conducive for the screening process of the candidate so you can expect to asked for a means of contact.

Another viable option when scouting candidates for immigration exploitation is the internet and online dating websites. Aside from being a powerful tool of educational value; the internet also serves as a source of entertainment, inclusive of: romance, dating and sometimes casual sex. The World Wide Web and social media offer a platform of plentiful pickings of prospective candidates, as do telephone chat lines in encountering the beautiful bimbos, voluptuous vixens to the ugly egore's – ready, willing, able to meet and greet.

In some cases, family or friends of the "in need immigrant" play match maker by introducing the "in need immigrant" to an unassuming American for exploitation. You may have a co –worker, neighbor, classmate or friend that may be privy to your single status and may claim to have the perfect partner for you. <u>Be weary and exercise</u>

caution, if and when you decide to be introduced as this could be a **_behavioral cue_** of a co-worker, neighbor, classmate or friend facilitating immigration fraud knowingly or unknowingly.

Once contact has been established and the candidate is receptive the hard work has been done and the bait has been set. And it is only a matter of getting the candidate of potential prey - hook (**love**), line (**leverage**) and sinker (**loss**). The next order in the process of the prospective candidate is the screening process.

THREE – SCREENING THE CANDIDATE

The intelligence of the immigrant and their motives, people and places of opportunity have been explored, explained - now the next component of the process of relationship exploitation and marriage fraud is the screening process of the "person of potential" (the candidate).

The relationship dynamic of the "in need immigrant" and an "unassuming American" has to be conducive to the needs of the immigrant and <u>meet or exceed the expectations, scrutiny of the Immigration and Naturalization Service</u>. The Immigration and Naturalization Service has been dismantled into three separate entities the: U.S Customs and Border Protection (CBP), U.S Immigration and Customs Enforcement (ICE) and the <u>U.S Citizenship and Immigration Services (USCIS), which focuses on marriage sponsorship and visas.</u>

<u>*Yet, the relationship has to seem symbiotic in meeting your emotional and relationship needs, wants.*</u> Once a prospective person of potential and interest (the candidate) has been met through a place of opportunity, next starts the screening process. You may find, once being approached you may be subjected to a barrage of questions that may seem meaningless or even intrusive, interrogative dependent upon your view of prospective.

The questions may be inclusive of relationship or marital status, inquiries of your family dynamic and employment status. Often single parents are ideal targets, as it assumed that there is a void to fill. The answers, if supplied by the candidate will determine if you are ideal match for the "in need immigrant" and whether or not, to proceed with the acquaintance in hopes of cultivating a relationship.

If you answer the questions and are determined to be an ideal candidate for exploitation, you will most likely be asked for a means of contact – this may include a phone number or social media platform (I.E: Facebook, Instagram, Twitter, YouTube etcetera). People in general have taken to social media. Social media has given a voice to the voiceless. People often express themselves and their emotions on social media – the good, bad, ugly, tasteless and tactless.

You would be astounded at the immigrant intelligence that the "in need immigrant" will use when viewing posts to adumbrate you and draw character conclusions, generalizations and identify insecurities, vulnerabilities from your posts within social media platforms – so be mindful of what you post and the accessible audience for your posts.

Once a form of contact has been established you will be contacted for conversation which may seem light hearted, as a way of disarming your defenses but will at some point revert back to screening questions. It is at the advantage of the "in need immigrant" to keep you in conciliation with your defenses down and to make you feel comfortable.

As a result you will likely be asked out on a date in a public setting. On the date you will likely be wooed with great manners, flowers, candy and perhaps a trinket – this is again, to diminish your defenses and put you at ease. You likely find the awkward and excruciating silence of a first date is off put with the charisma the "in need immigrant" exudes in conversation - peppered with occasional rapid fire questioning throughout the discourse. This is also a form of Motivational Interviewing for a prospective candidate.

In some cases, the "in need immigrant" will listen more than talk to gain insight and allow you to expose your insecurities, vulnerabilities - one layer, at a time.

While the "in need immigrant" is agog with attention and asking questions - **you may find that your _own_ questions about their relationship/marital status, employment status, family dynamic and immigration status etcetera are dismissed coyly or answered with vague answers or may seem to be embellished.** An immigrant will not likely divulge their immigration status at such a premature stage in the courtship.

However - if there is a meeting of minds in respect to receptiveness and reciprocation you will be asked out again which affords the opportunity for further acquaintance, questioning in hopes of cultivating a relationship.

As the acquaintance between the two of you progresses, so will the screening questions – becoming more assertive, direct. You may find you are asked, if you have: ever be arrested, prosecuted and convicted of a crime, filed taxes, your immigration status (citizen by birth or naturalization), if you have been divorced and if so, how long ago or are you or were a public assistance recipient in any capacity (food stamps, Medicaid)??!! **Aggressive questioning is a _behavioral cue_.**

This questioning is "purposeful purging" of information from you. By aggressively asking questioning the "in need immigrant" is able to gauge your candidacy as a sponsor. Because if you are a U.S citizen with a criminal background who has never filed taxes and are on public assistance; you wouldn't fit the criteria of a sponsor for immigration purposes and the "in need immigrant" would be move on to the next candidate.

The "in need immigrant" is able to morph into who and what you need or want in a relationship, so be mindful in what you discuss and answer when asked specific questions.

Presuming you meet the criteria; as a prospective candidate for immigration relationship exploitation and marriage fraud gauged by your responses to the "in need immigrant's" questions - fitting not only the needs of the "in need immigrant" but also the criteria specified by the U.S Citizenship and Immigration Services (USCIS), *allows for the continuity of your new acquaintance or relationship to flourish.*

FOUR - COURTSHIP, DATING

So you've met, answered questions that have deemed you the right fit for the positions you play, the "in need immigrant" and the "unassuming American". Now starts the ritualistic courtship and dating, which will be a catalyst for the next phases of your relationship - cultural, religious exploitation and the improper proposition of marriage, which will be discussed in Chapters 5 and 6, respectively.

Courtship and dating is a crucial component of the scam by penetrating your defenses, in effort to exploit them. As with erecting any building - foundation is key. The same can be said for dating, courtship - as the foundation of both, set the tone for the relationship. Allowing a relationship to thrive or dive, in a plummet.

At such a pivotal phase of the scam of exploitation; having gathered their own immigrant intelligence on applicable immigration programs, visas etcetera and having found the ideal candidate - "you" and now having insight into your insecurities and vulnerabilities through both motivational interviewing and purposeful purging. They aren't going to lose you now if they can help it. Hence, dating and courtship.

You can expect to have your emotional needs met with the accessibility of the "in need immigrant". You can expect your angst to be put at ease. You can expect assiduous attention. You can expect to be wooed, romanced, wined and dined beyond your wildest dreams. Your date(s) will be anything but predictable.

The "in need immigrant" will be a purveyor of passion as I've heard stories of fairytale first dates of horse drawn carriage rides in the park and being serenaded. Additionally, some of my most memorable dates were with my then immigrant husbands. Flowers, food, gifts, attention, accessibility, conversation and companionship are all at your disposal - as you are being baited into a parasitic relationship for personal profit, gain and exploitation.

The cost comparison of a few quality dates of dinner and a museum such as an art exhibit or a carriage ride over the mundane dinner and a movie date – versus' the cost of $10,000.00 to $30,000 for an arranged business marriage or border crossing is seemingly equitable tradeoff. The **choice** is easy for the "in need immigrant" and minimal in cost comparison to their potential earning ability as a, green card visa holder.

Realize that there is no expense that the "in need immigrant" will spare - in regards to time, accessibility and monetary value within their budget to get you hook (**love**), line (**leverage**) and sinker (**loss**).

It is not just about making an impression on you but also making an impression on the important people in your life - family and friends is just as important. The "in need immigrant" may ask to meet your family and friends early onset. They may introduce you to *limited* and *selective* family and friends of theirs, as well. I've both experienced and heard stories of "in need immigrants" misrepresenting the true relationship of family members and friends, so beware.

They may refer to friends as a specific family member, such as a: brother, sister or cousin. In some situations, they may have a friend of the opposite sex that they may claim is a relative, such as a cousin – when in reality they are "kissing cousins" and "special friends with benefits".

Often you will not be able to vet and verify the validity and true nature of an extended family member or friend – so it is important to use both *observatory and behavioral cues*, such as body language and inflection in the tone of voice when they speak to family members or friends to help gauge these relationships.

The introduction process is to assure you that they interested in you, foresee a long term relationship with you. It may also be a way to gauge your family and friends influence - as family and friends could have a bearing on the relationship be it positively or negatively.

You may find that that when you are out and about on your date(s) that your suitor tends to make every moment with you, a Kodak moment with pictures and cellphone selfie's while claiming to be in awe with you or that they are falling in love with you. Claims of strong feelings of lust are to be expected. Some may even make proclamations of love which should be interpreted as too much, too soon. Taking excessive amounts of photos every outing is a *behavioral cue* of immigration relationship exploitation, you should be cognizant of. While taking photos may seem innocent, sentimental and reminiscent of your courtship and dates often there are driven motives for such as actions.

Photographs create a photographic timeline of your courtship and relationship for immigration purposes with the U.S Citizenship and Immigration Services (USCIS) which facilitates marriage sponsorship and visas.

Men of manners and women of virtue are what are exhibited at all times. Expect the "in need immigrant" in their Sunday's best when out and about – shirt and tie, suits, hard bottom shoes, high heels and quality professional looking attire. This is to be conspicuous, appear to have measurable success gauged by their dapper appearance or designer clothes.

What seemed at the inception of your acquaintance to be Mr. Right Now or Ms. Right Now - now seems more like Mr. Right or Ms. Right by seeming sublime.

Purposeful purging; allowed for your innermost thoughts, emotions, insecurities and vulnerabilities to be exposed for exploitation unassumingly through what _you thought_ was light hearted conversation and questioning in getting to know someone – as, it is their ability to assimilate to your relationship needs, wants.

It is important to exercise your own immigrant intelligence so that you do not abnegate your visa sponsorship ability to the venal lure of a few kind words, a few five dollar bouquets of flowers and a couple of hot meals at a restaurant (such as my experience) would be abysmal.

With a parasite, a host is needed and an environment to thrive. The "in need immigrant" is such a parasite and the environment of the U.S is where they want to live, thrive and "you" are the host.

Progression has taken shape; acquaintance has led to a relationship and infatuation to feelings of lust and maybe even love at this point. A caveat to heed is that the cultural and religious beliefs and views of the "in need immigrant" can also be used to exploit you. And will be explained in the next chapter.

FIVE - CULTURAL, RELIGIOUS EXPLOITATION

Your acquaintance has now progressed into a relationship. At this point - you may or may not have developed a rapport with your significant other, the "in need immigrant" where you are privy to their immigration status. However, your partner the "in need immigrant" may be loquacious and discuss a future together- *your* hopes and dreams. You may have also, discussed relationship goals, long term goals and even children. Often, the "in need immigrant" will be guarded when discussing their own specific goals – as, being with you is sojourn and will not be protracted. A relationship and marriage long term with you isn't likely part of their goals.

And with any relationship, influences of family and friends – as well, as cultural and religious beliefs and views will be factored in. **To reiterate, it is important that you are aware of the specific country of origin and the cultural, religious influences of their people.**

Don't expect to be invited to many or any cultural events or religious events, especially if you are of a different faith because it would be of great concern to the "in need immigrant" if you were to hear or see something objectionable that would cause conflict with your own values, beliefs and ultimately put the relationship at risk.

Recognize that despite wanting to reside in the U.S legally, as a green card visa holder or citizen – most immigrants and immigrant communities are insular. And most immigrants will feel comfortable amongst their own people that subscribe to their cultural beliefs, views and will often gravitate to areas where their people are majority not the minority. Hence - China town, Little Italy both in lower Manhattan and Little Senegal in Harlem.

The relationship may move at a fast pace, however the introduction of sex may be purposely premature. The dynamic of sex will be influenced by individual preferences, cultural, religious beliefs and views.

Sex can be a beautiful expression of an emotional connection and union between two consenting adults. However, sex can also be a tool of manipulation and exploitation.

You may find that "in need immigrant" you are involved with seems to have a transcendental relationship with their God, may attend religious services regularly and may pray multiple times a day. Don't let their sanctimonious acts of faith in observing their religion dismay you – the "in need immigrant" while seeming devoutly religious is specious and you can, probably will be exploited without conscience as all religions of faith offer forgiveness for devious acts. Just as some "convenient Christians" lie and commit bad acts - even some devout Muslims subscribe to the practice of Al-Taqiyya (the Arabic word for dissimulation, noting deceit as a "Holy Deception"). No matter the religion, the "in need immigrant" has the ability to misrepresent their agenda and motives when dating you with lies, deceit and will.

The "in need immigrant" may be distinguished and decorous, deeply enmeshed with their religion and may even wear an amulet around their neck or waist – this particularly true of African, West Indian and Muslim immigrants but these practices will vary by country of origin, religion and personal preference. Many West Indian, African and Muslim immigrants have a spiritual advisor that they seek advisement from for many life areas, including love and marriage in addition to the designated God of their faith.

You might find the "in need immigrant" may exhibit decorum while expressing amorous admiration towards you but doesn't press the issue of having sex, again this is purposeful and a methodical part of the scam. As most, religions adhere to sex being reserved for married couples. But for some people sex is a component of a romantic relationship, married or not.

Once you've dated and been courted, sex may seem like a natural uncomplicated progression. But when dealing with "in need immigrant" nothing on the surface is uncomplicated.

You may have a developed a perceived level of trust and monogamy with the "in need immigrant" where you have progressed to sexual intercourse but aren't practicing safe sex. The fore mentioned discussions and abstinence of safe sex practices, could be a ploy to have you become impregnated and put you in a position of compromise should a unplanned pregnancy arise for marriage. A pregnancy resulting in a child would be the ideal circumstance to facilitate a formal legally recognized marriage proposal.

After multiple episodes of consummation of the relationship through sex, the "in need immigrant" may claim your sensuality made them depraved and that they have defiled their religion by engaging in sexual acts while being unmarried. They may claim that the only rectification is to have a cultural ceremony, religious ceremony or a religious marriage and may refuse to have further sexual relations with you unless you remit to their request.

You might hear the word, marriage and either be ready to run for the hills *or* run to the alter. The **choice** of whether to run for the hills or run to the alter, is a matter of personal preference.

It is worth mentioning any suggestion of a cultural ceremony, religious ceremony or religious marriage should be met with skepticism as such, a suggestion is a **behavioral cue** of escalation of the relationship when you're dating and courting, while still getting to know each other.

The "in need immigrant" will likely inveigle you with reassurance that the cultural ceremony, religious ceremony or religious marriage is not a formality or recognized legally but merely, for the cultural and religious observances of *their* religion and/or culture - essentially being for them not you.

The cunning and crafty ways the "in need immigrant" know no boundary, not even of religious proportion. Acceptance of their terms of a cultural ceremony, religious ceremony or religious marriage opens the door for further exploitation and **is an integral part of the scam of immigration relationship exploitation and marriage fraud.** Your acceptance of **_any_** cultural ceremony**,** religious ceremony or religious marriage in any capacity is indicative of your commitment to them and readiness for next step of the scam – which is to propose a legally recognized marriage to you formally. Claims of strong feelings of love alluding to marriage, even if only recognized culturally or religiously within the community of the "in need immigrant" is a **behavioral cue** to cognizant of – too much too soon.

Being accessible to you and exhibiting that they are there for you is of heightened importance. Dates, long days and late nights together now lead to overnight stays. Slowly, usually one article of possession at a time they begin to stake claim on you and your domain, your home. Before you realize it, you're living together as husband and wife. And the compos mentis effect begins.

SIX - IMPROPER PROPOSITION (MARRIAGE)

Compos Mentis is total control of one's mind. The "in need immigrant" has both your family and friends *and* their family and friends aligned (they are very important, as they may be asked to submit written statements of acknowledgment of your relationship, union to immigration should you accept the proposal and marry legally), your body, presence in your home and now your mind - by having **control** of your emotions with strong entranced feelings of lust, love.

After time elapses, within the relationship and you're feeling content, comfortable you likely will be coaxed or supplicated into an improper proposal of formal marriage. I refer to the proposal as an "improper proposal" because the proposal is often generated out of need - the "in need immigrant" wants to stay in the U.S when other visa options have been exhausted and needs to marry an unassuming American - "you" to sponsor their visa.

Love and marriage, there should be a correlation between the two but when involved with the "in need immigrant" often, you will find love is an afterthought. The primary thought process of the "in need immigrant" is to propose a legally recognized marriage for immigration sponsorship purposes.

You've been wooed, romanced, wined and dined. You've progressed from an acquaintance to a relationship. You and your significant other in a union of sorts, be it culturally and/or religiously recognized. You're co-habiting, living together as husband and wife. Now you're about to be bamboozled into a legally recognized marriage and they are about to make the transition from "in need immigrant" to migrant and green visa holder.

They've been attentive, affectionate and accessible – appearing more to be the Mr. Right or Ms. Right that you've sought. They may be making monetary contributions to the household and dutiful with household chores like cooking, cleaning - presenting themselves more and more as the ideal mate and spouse. The "in need immigrant" may offer to pay household bills such as cable or utilities, in addition to their monetary contribution but insist that their name be placed on accounts. This is another **purposeful ploy** of the "in need immigrant".

Now seems like an ideal time for the "in need immigrant" to be candid with you about their immigration status, if they haven't already. This disclosure is also purposeful.

As an illegal immigrant, work opportunities are available but the pay may not be competitive or even at the minimum wage rate - that is why it is purposeful for the disclosure of their immigration status as it leads to opening a discussion of the financial responsibilities of a spouse.

They may make claims about how they love you endlessly, want to be able to provide for you as their spouse **but** their immigration status prohibits them from accessing better paying jobs to provide for you accordingly.

They aren't going to come out and game you with lines like "Baby I Love you so much, marry me so I can get my green card". The "in need immigrant" will be subtle in approach **or** even suggestive, they will make their proposal based on purported love, care, concern for you and a way of being a better spouse by being a provider for you.

Remember, it will always be about "you" or "us", as a focal point - never about them as an individual, <u>at this stage in the immigration scam.</u>

Once you have accepted the proposal of the "in need immigrant" you may be urged to set a date as soon as possible. The ideal and most likely, suggested venue for the wedding will be at your local government building, such as your local city or town hall or county clerk's office in a legally recognized civil ceremony. **<u>So don't expect much planning or preparation</u>** <u>– other than coordinating a date that is conducive for the supporting cast of family and friends to attend, as they will likely serve as witnesses of the marriage ceremony and additionally supply affidavit statements to immigration in a double duty of sorts.</u>

The urging of setting a date as soon as possible in a civil ceremony setting are both ***behavioral cues***.

This type of civil ceremony is a legal marriage more so than a religiously based marriage. The suggestion of a civil ceremony is purposeful as some officiants such as preachers, etcetera may not have the proper credentials required in your state to officiate a marriage that will be legally recognized.

Let's keep things in prospective – You're looking for love and their looking for help.

SEVEN - IMMIGRATION FILING, SPONSORSHIP

You have dated, had a religious or culturally recognized ceremony and now you've accepted the marriage proposal of your significant other-the "in need immigrant". You set the date for your civil ceremony, invited guests of family and friends and now you are about to become a legally recognized spouse. The date came and went; now you are a legally recognized spouse and now you're about become a legally recognized immigration visa sponsor of your husband or wife.

Soon after your now legally recognized marriage ceremony, you might be urged to file immigration sponsorship forms and secure an appointment with your local immigration office for an interview. The reasons for the urgency may vary and the "in need immigrant" may stick to the script with claims of being able to provide you as their spouse by being able to find a better paying job once obtaining their green card visa. Or the "in need immigrant" may play on your emotions with claims that he or she can deported anytime, that they couldn't bare being separated from you.

In my case of Immigration marriage fraud, one of husbands began to cry to elicit empathy from me for his cause. Tears from the "in need immigrant" are to be expected and you will soon cry your own from pain or pleasure during your involvement with the "in need immigrant" – but you will cry.

During this critical time of immigration sponsorship filing you may find the frequency and duration of presumable love making (sex) with the "in need immigrant" may increase. This maybe in attempt to become pregnant, as a now "legally recognized" marriage that produces a pregnancy resulting in a child would solidify the marriage with immigration officials. Care of the child should the marriage dissolve, much like love within the marriage is an after-thought.

In some cases the "in need immigrant" may ask you to front them the application fees with promises to repay you in full once gainful employment is secured after their visa is issued. But poor planning and lack of preparation didn't get the "in need immigrant" this far into the scam of relationship exploitation and marriage fraud. While urging you file the documents and to secure an appointment with immigration officials the "in need immigrant" may disclose that they can pay all applicable filing fees putting you at ease, by absolving you of any financial hardship.

During this time you can continuously expect to be imbued with feelings of love, respect and value. And you are a valuable commodity of acquisition, as a legally recognized green card visa sponsoring spouse. You can expect the date nights, flowers, gifts and surprises to continue. They will still be very accessible to you, checking in with calls and texts in their physical absence and continue to make every moment spent together with you, a Kodak moment by taking pictures.

It is important at this stage to keep you happy, content and not exhibit any change in behavior. **The "in need immigrant" maybe overly affectionate and tell that they love you repeatedly, it is important that they purport claims of love for you and that you feel that they love you for you and not your sponsoring status as their spouse**.

Once the immigration papers have been filed, the date of the immigration interview has been secured the "in need immigrant" might revert back to aggressive questioning tactics in preparation of possible random questioning by immigration officials. The day of the interview, you can expect for your hand to be held or your face, hair to be gently stroked and comfortable conversation, drivel that extracts a smile or laugh from you, as you both anxiously wait to be called in by immigration officials for the interview.

After the filing and interview, presuming you passed the scrutiny of immigration officials the "in need immigrant" has now transitioned into a migrant green card visa holder. Or what I refer to as the "master manipulator" or "manipulative migrant", but for the sake of content I shall use the term **"manipulative migrant"**.

The "manipulative migrant" may offer to open a bank account or ask that you place them as an authorized user on credit cards – this purposeful in demonstrating to immigration officials in the future, that you share financial responsibility and liability as husband and wife by co-mingling finances.

During the two or three year status of issuance of the green card visa you may start to see either small or big changes that have negatively impacted your relationship and marriage. Likely this because the statute of limitations has been met in terms of immigration marriage requirements - you have already supplied what was needed to substantiate the marriage in terms of documents such as: bills, accounts with both your names, a lease, life or medical insurance documents etcetera and attended immigration appointments as their supportive spouse.

Now you are entering the twilight zone of the beginning of the end of your relationship and marriage to the "manipulative migrant".

EIGHT - THE END OF THE BEGINNING

Admit it, your relationship is now undeniably on the rocks and *"your"* presumable marital bliss is gone. You as the supportive spouse and green card visa sponsor don't understand what happened or what went awry – he or she just isn't doing the things they used to and treating you like they used to. There is a noticeable shift in your relationship and marriage. Your relationship and marriage is going to hell in a hand basket.

You've been "put on pause"- the check in calls, texts may have stopped altogether or become infrequent. The dates, flowers and gifts may stop or also, may have become less frequent as well. The "manipulative migrant" may start spending less time with you and more time away from the marital home with late nights and early mornings. Thus - becoming less accessible to you.

Intimacy for the "manipulative migrant" may now seem like a chore or be nonexistent. They may claim to be "at work" when in all actuality they are "working it" with other women or men. As I had the experience of discovering online dating profiles of one of my husbands soliciting sex and companionship from other women - in which he claimed he was single and never married during our marriage.

They may have become more guarded - hiding money in <u>now</u> secret and separate bank accounts. They may talk late and often in hushed tones in their native language on the phone – but the language of truth, is foreign to them. They may put a lock on their cellular phone or remove photo's of you from their social media accounts or restrict your access. They may become invective and act jibe towards you.

You are probably in disbelief, feeling forgotten, dejected and rejected. And who wouldn't when such a noticeable shift in your relationship and marriage has occurred.

Allow me to give insight, into what has happened – you have officially been used, devalued, disrespected and will be disposed of. What you didn't want to believe was the motivation for your marriage (a green card visa and/or citizenship) is clearly defined and outlined by behaviors, actions and sometimes by the words of "manipulative migrant" that are indicative that you have been victimized and that you are in fact, a victim of marriage fraud for immigration purposes.

You have met the burden of proof for the *once* "in need immigrant" and _now_ "manipulative migrant" – whom now is, your legally recognized spouse and a green card visa holder presumably with ambitions of citizenship. But most importantly, you have met the burden of proof for U.S Citizenship and Immigration Services (USCIS).

Their actions, behaviors may implore to you lose **control** of your emotions and react harshly in a confrontational matter of domestic dispute. It is important to make a conscience **choice** to exercise restraint and harness your emotions; as the desperation of the "manipulative migrant" to stay in the U.S by any means necessary - may involve calling law enforcement on you to maintain their green card visa status by using any incident of perceived aggression as a clause for a change in their immigration visa application, as a victim of domestic violence. The "in need immigrant" has a propensity for perjury as he or she, has lied to both you and U.S Citizenship and Immigration Services (USCIS) – lying to the police and filing a false report is of, no exception.

Thus having you become embroiled in legal matters (police statements, orders of protection, court dates etcetera) and financial woes (bail, attorney retainer fees, days missed at work etcetera). By reacting adversely, you would be giving the "manipulative migrant" an "out" - that he or she wasn't man or woman enough to say that they wanted.

Don't do it!! If you truly believe you are a victim of marriage fraud explore other viable options such as contacting your local immigration office and elected local officials such the District Attorney's Office. But be forewarned, often these government agencies have a lackadaisical approach to the seriousness of this silent epidemic. And are often inundated with large volumes of immigration marriage fraud complaints and your complaint may not take precedence or even warrant a personal response.

That is why it is imperative that you become your own advocate by listening to your inner voice when something seems off and by recognizing the behavioral cues of such parasitic people and master manipulators, such as the: "in need immigrant" and "manipulative migrant".

Someone has to be blamed and someone has to play the fool, sadly you found out too little – too late that you have played the fool in an immigration relationship and marriage scam. You may blame yourself. Pondering, how could you be so foolish??!! You have invested time, money, emotions and resources - **but more importantly your heart** into a parasitic relationship with the once "in need immigrant" and now, "manipulative migrant".

It is easy to blame yourself; as it is likely the "manipulative migrant" is probably blaming you for the breakdown in the relationship and marriage and defaming your name with his or her family, friends. **"Deflecting and redirecting"** their unconscionable culpability by projecting blame unto you without any feelings of compunction.

It is important to seek the support of family, friends and/or seek professional help if needed.

The Mr. Right or Ms. / Mrs. Right that you thought was a blessing - taught you a painful lesson on **love**, **leverage** and *now* **loss.**

 Loss, of what <u>you thought</u> the dynamic of your relationship and marriage was and **loss**, of trust now that you know what the *true* dynamic and basis of your relationship and marriage, is or was.

Welcome to the Heartbreak hotel, come on in - the water is warm and check-in is at right.

NINE - SEPERATION, DIVORCE & HEALING THE HURT

Language, cultural and religious differences can be a barrier for anyone and cause certain strain on a marriage - even a marriage of fraud and opportunity. Yet, in spite of the fore-mentioned for months or years, someway somehow – you were able to hold it together.

But now, ironically after the statute of limitations for their immigration visa marital filing has lapsed – suddenly the things that held you together tear you apart. At this point, the love you thought you had is extinguished and the strain and distance between the two of you within your marriage may have reached the pinnacle where it is irrevocably broken. Most likely, your spouse has decided to separate from you as their self-serving needs have been fulfilled and you are now disposable. Divorce is now an explorable option.

Lines that once seemed blurred are now drawn and sides taken – you _now_ know with certainty, the one you love was faking. The "manipulative migrant" has been faking love, emotion, care and concern.

As the vicissitudes of life, past relationships and now your failed marriage come into focus. Rivulets of tears and the formulation of irrational thoughts may now be constant and consuming. You are a victim of marriage fraud and are experiencing a **loss**. You have experienced **loss** of love, **loss** of your spouse and **loss** of your marriage. And with any **loss**, you must allow yourself time to "process the pain" and grieve.

Immigration relationship exploitation and marriage fraud leaves an indelible mark of memory on those affected. Often causing incendiary feelings, that make the victims of this crime of opportunity feel incensed.

How do you silence the immutable echoes of the questions you may ask yourself (or is this just me): Why did this happen to me? What did I do to deserve this? Why doesn't he or she love me like I love him or her? How can I make him or her love me? How could I be so dumb? How could I be so foolish? How could my husband or wife dispose of me, as if I was yesterday's trash?

While all these questions are of merit, the most important questions that you should ask yourself are: How do I go from victim to victor? How do I learn to love and trust again? Now, that your spouse has moved on with their green card visa but without you.

So what- now what??!! This maybe your thought process at this point. **Realization and acceptance is everything.** Life and negative experiences can either **"build you up or break you down"**. To be built up or broken down is a matter of **choice**.

I know how it feels to be: angry and hurt with feelings of being used, thrown away. I know how it feels to be depressed and oppressed. I know about **loss**. The **loss** of the love you thought you had, the **loss** of trust and feeling violated once you realize you have been exploited in marriage fraud.

During one of my marriages - in the time span of one year I lost two babies and my husband, though it was only his permanent physical presence as he had abandoned me and marriage emotionally, financially long ago. The **loss** of my babies, the **loss** of my husband whom I loved like no other man - the **loss** of yearning for that idyllic life that I wanted with my husband made me have irrational thoughts of suicide.

I didn't want just a wedding - I wanted a loving, nurturing, supportive marriage with both of my husbands. I wanted a family and babies, not a roommate or baby daddy. I wanted so desperately, a future with my husbands. But I didn't get my "happily ever after" so I can tell you- I know about emotional pain, **loss** and I don't want to experience anymore of it.

I made the **choice** to let the experiences of **both** marriages build me up. **I decided to make the rest of my life - the best of my life.**

Life goes on with you or without you. When life kicks your ass, it may be hard to "move past the pain" and have the fortitude to forge forward <u>but you must.</u>

The first thing you must do is kill those **<u>A.N.T's</u>** in your head and your ear. A.N.T's you say??!! Yes, A.N.T's - not insects, but those **<u>Automatic Negative Thoughts</u>**.

Stop blaming yourself, **stop** apologizing, **stop** doubting yourself with real or perceived fears of failure or inadequacy, **stop** caring about people that don't care about you, **stop** allowing yourself to be used, devalued and disrespected, **stop** going along to get along, **stop** being so accessible, **stop** stressing over the small stuff and **<u>stop all communication with husband or wife that defrauded you into marriage for immigration purposes.</u>** Just stop it all!!

You can't change your opinion of yourself having pity parties wallowing insecurities, self-doubt and self-defeat. Self-love, like love projected unto you by others is a process and will always be deficient unless you actively work at it. So start "getting into you" and get out and get about.

I understand - though illogical, that despite being used, defrauded and disposed of you might still have love in your heart for your former spouse as, I still have love for one of my husbands too. Spank me. But as my grandmother Betty, used to say to her husband - **"I love you but I love me more and I can love you from a distance". But really it is time to move on – "get over yourself" because your husband or wife already has.**

Remove the reminders of memories made with your ex- take down the photos, remove their number from your phone, move, change the furniture, get rid of the trinkets and mementos. Just as it took time to fall in love, it will take time to fall out of love. Allow yourself time to heal and process the pain.

Humans are resilient, resourceful and in some cases repairable. While you might not love or trust like you once did – you can and will learn to love again without being used and trust again without being naïve. Presumably with exercised caution you will learn to love, trust again - unless you choose otherwise, now that you are privy to the modus operandi and behavioral cues that may signal a potential problem(s) in your relationship.

But encouraged, it can be done – on your own or with the support and care of others. You have been through a traumatic experience and need, deserve support. Tough times don't last long but tough people do – you went into your marriage in good faith, it was him or her that did wrong. Don't give up, you're too strong.

Family and friends can help render emotional support, though I can understand that this may not a first choice for many people. Especially, if you had naysayers when you first began dating and getting serious with your relationship. No one likes to hear "I told you so".

Medical professionals such as a therapist or psychologist can offer a safe space to talk in comfort and confidence, provided you aren't making comments deemed to be homicidal or suicidal thoughts. A psychiatrist, who can dispense medication to help with the incredible sadness, you may be experiencing from either diagnosed or undiagnosed depression associated with the **loss** of your love and marriage can be another source of help when healing the hurt.

Many communities have local support groups for the single, separated and/or divorced. Support groups are often free – but, please no rebound dating within these groups.

You can learn to love yourself that means taking time for reflection and taking accountability, if needed. Learning to embrace and accept yourself as is, flaws and all – and recognizing that you can be flawed and still be fabulous. **Actively working on what you can change and letting go what you cannot.** You can lose weight, fix your teeth or other physical attributes - if your health care insurance and budget permits but <u>**you can't make someone love you that doesn't *or* never did - no matter what you think, heard or read.**</u>

Reconnecting to recreational activities (and I don't mean drinking and drugging, if that was your scene) can help serve as a distraction when healing the hurt. Maybe you liked to ride bikes *or* fly model air planes *or* paint - but with the hustle and bustle of work, family or school you lost interest. Now is a good time to become reintroduced.

Maybe you never took the time to know what you recreational activities you like – take a crochet class or watch a YouTube "How to" video.

Make things happen instead of waiting for them to happen by finding solutions instead of excuses. Go back to school or get a new career focus. Volunteer, I know this may sound bad but nothing will make you better about your circumstances with a positive prospective than being around people who have it worse. Misery doesn't always like company but sometimes the bitch likes to peer in, say hi.

But in all seriousness, other people are often critical and life is hard enough – kicking ass and asking no questions. We must not abuse ourselves or allow others to use us. Be gentle with yourself and know you are not alone in the shared experience of Immigration marriage fraud. Forgive yourself and try to forgive those that have hurt, used and discarded you. Love the life you have and try to create the life you want.

Be well and don't give up or don't give in.

Contact

For Interviews, Speaking Engagements, Work Shops, Signed Book Copies, Business Offers of Monetary Value, Movie Right Inquiries <u>Only</u> contact the Author, Andrea M.V. Hunter – Diop via Email at: <u>FAHunterHeritage@Yahoo.com</u>

For General Inquiries and Comments via Email at: <u>LoveLeverageLoss@Yahoo.com</u> <u>though your comments and questions are welcomed and appreciated, a response is not guaranteed.</u>

Stay Connected

Facebook - LoveLeverageLoss Thebook

www.ingramcontent.com/pod-product-compliance
Lightning Source LLC
Chambersburg PA
CBHW080533030426

42337CB00023B/4710